MW00982384

Dusk to Dusk

Reflections of the Spirit
and Seasons of Love

Michael B. Poyntz
aka
'Irish'

Includes a preview selection of soon to be released 'Dawn to Dawn' featuring the acclaimed poems 'Cloudy Skies', 'Gifts Within Your Lifetime' plus the emotional tribute 'Let the Mercy Begin' dedicated to the New York City Fire Department.

Copyright © 2010 by Michael B. Poyntz
First Edition – April 2010

ISBN
978-1-77067-024-2 (Paperback)
978-1-77067-025-9 (eBook)

Cover photo by Alex Dodin.
Editing and revising by David Soy.
"Ankle Deep" co-written by Emily Manno.

All rights reserved.

No part of this publication may be reproduced in any form,
or by any means, electronic or mechanical, including photocopy-
ing, recording, or any information browsing, storage, or retrieval
system, without permission in writing from the publisher.

This book contains various excerpts from the forthcoming collection 'Dawn
to Dawn' by Michael B. Poyntz aka 'Irish' as well as poems now appearing
worldwide in the 'That Canadian Poet' Imagine Poster series! Some poem
excerpts have been set for this edition of 'Dusk to Dusk' only and may
not reflect the final contents of the forthcoming sequel or posters.

'Dusk to Dusk', 'That Canadian Poet' poster series and 'Dawn
to Dawn' are works of fiction and no poem is a reflection of any
person nor circumstance related to any person or place.

∞

Published by:

Suite 300 – 777 Fort Street
Victoria, BC, Canada V8W 1G9
www.friesenpress.com

For information on bulk orders contact:
info@friesenpress.com or fax 1-888-376-7026
Distributed to the trade by The Ingram Book Company

WHAT READERS ARE SAYING ABOUT
Michael B. Poyntz 'DUSK TO DUSK' Poetry Collection

"As good as it gets in contemporary romantic poetry-
Irish is writing at the top of his game"

KA, Victoria, BC, Canada

"Awesome, he catches you off guard with poem after poem
exploring the highs and lows of life and romance!"

AD, Nanoose, BC, Canada

"I was able to whisper 'Evermore' into my husbands ear on
our 35th anniversary! Thanks for a wonderful gift."

GH, Edmonton, Alberta, Canada

"Love the poem Cloudy Skies. We often study the clouds above and around us
and find worlds and dreams and people and whole stories contained in these
fragile scapes, and thus can easily relate to your thoughts in these words."

DS , Gabriola Island, BC, Canada

"Makes you laugh, then cry, then smile again! I loved this book!"

RW, Toronto, Ont., Canada

"The poem 'Double Dog Dare Ya' made me think of my childhood best
friend and inspired me to track him down! Today, we are once again 'Best
friends forever', what else would we be? Thank you for the inspiration."

MP, San Jose, Calif., USA

"Michael wrote the poem 'My Hero's Song' while sitting beside me on a
plane to give to my father who was dying! In his thirty years my father had
never been able to say the words 'I love you'. After reading 'My Hero's Song'
my father held me in his arms whispering the words 'I love you, I love you'.
What can I say, Michael, thank you forever from the bottom of my heart!"

Marlo, Vancouver, BC, Canada

WHAT CRITICS ARE SAYING ABOUT
Michael B Poyntz 'DUSK TO DUSK' Poetry Collection

An outstanding contemporary collection of poems about love - from a lover to a lover, a parent to a child, a grandmother to her grandchild, a nation to its fallen firemen. From those that have fallen in love at "Hello"! The poems 'Cloudy Skies' and 'On the Rocks' are unique examples of extraordinary metaphoric writing! The exquisite poem Dusk to Dusk 'Passion' will tug at the very pulse of your heartbeat. Lovers and their Soul-Mates are universal beings! We may walk to a different beat in time- but love, true love can cross all barriers! Through a landscape of over 70 poems this collection will capture readers of many ages and cultures.

Dusk to Dusk

Reflections of the Spirit and Seasons of Love

Michael B. Poyntz
aka
'Irish'

Authors Acknowledgments

Author Disclaimer: Please note that I write utilizing a 'free verse' format and as such DO NOT adhere to standard punctuation rules or spacing. Use of either upper or lower case is at my writer's discretion.

After three decades or more of madly scribbling various notes, poems and lyrics on dinner napkins around the world I have managed to almost run out of friends willing to offer comments or other about my poems. Indeed, 'Dusk to Dusk' is my response to the ongoing cajoling "You must write a book someday"! Voila! That day has arrived!

I have taken full measure of the poet's license to write as I felt the poems flow, including irregular spacing and incorrect punctuation. It is my way to try to catch the emotion that I felt as I wrote that poem. I hope that I have not offended too many purists and have opened the door to the reader to interpret my collection as they feel it!

A book is never the work of one person and 'Dusk to Dusk' is no exception! Truth be told there are too many people to adequately thank who have contributed in some way to what you are holding in your hands.

Emily Manno of Washington, D.C. co-wrote the poems 'Ankle Deep' and 'I Miss You' with me all on one lazy Sunday afternoon in August 2008. Emily is a truly talented and artistic poet of amazing depth and beauty. Her future in creative writing will, I am sure, become legendary.

David Soy of Gabriola Island, B.C. performed the editorial task with patience and an uncanny sense of wit and humour. He is a perfectionist when it comes to grammar and he went through countless yellow highlighter pens along the way. But David is IN NO WAY responsible for my Irish stubborn willpower attesting to leave the erratic spacing and odd use of lower case when we all know UPPER case lettering was in order.

All photographs and/or illustrations used herein were acquired under outright purchase or extended lease/royalty basis and are used with all rights reserved.

I truly hope that you enjoy 'Dusk to Dusk' and hopefully take the time to visit my website www.ThatCanadianPoet.com to view my entire collection of poems, scrolls and posters.

Michael B Poyntz, aka 'Irish'
Qualicum Bay, British Columbia, Canada
thatcanadianpoet@shaw.ca

Dedicated to Nicole B.

Who inspired the poem 'How' and every heartbeat since with countless smiles, laughter and the odd glass of amazing wine captured within hours of equally fascinating conversation!

Nicole, you are truly that one in a million!

TABLE OF CONTENTS

TABLE OF CONTENTS con't

Dusk to Dusk

Spring

Reflections of the Spirit and Seasons of Love

How

How far would you travel to find your own truths
If there were no borders and no one to stop you

How old would you wish to be
If only you counted your years or candles

How long would you hold on to me
If letting go meant farewell forever

How long would you care for the opinions of others
If your mirror reflected no conscience

How close would you dance
If the only music heard was my heartbeat

How long would you be faithful
If it depended on your word alone

How deeply could you love
If passion gave you everything but guaranteed nothing

How long would you stand by the one you love
If it meant standing against all odds

How much of you would you risk
If loving someone was truly dangerous

How long would you wait for me
If I promised to return someday

How sweetly would you sing
If only the deaf were listening

How long could you truly love
If love demanded only the truth

How much of me should I surrender to rescue you
If there is nothing in it for me

Irish

How - Lyrics

How old would you wish to be
if only you counted the candles on the cake
how long would you hold on to your soul
if all that you valued vanished once you let go
how far would you travel to discover your truths
if there were no one and no borders to stop you
how long would you care for the opinions of others
if your mirror reflected no conscience

How much of you would you risk to rescue me
if my heart was floating within a tangled destiny
how true are your words promising truth and trust
when words of all the others have ground belief to dust

How close would you dance in the arms of a moonbeam
if the only music heard was your heartbeat
how long would you be faithful
if it depended on trust alone
how deep would you love
if passion fulfilled everything and guaranteed nothing
how long would you stand by the one you love
if it meant standing against all odds

How much of you would you truly risk
if loving someone was truly dangerous
how long would you wait for someone
who promised to return someday
how sweetly would you sing
if only the deaf were listening
how long could you truly love
if love demanded nothing but the truth

If you heard my cry in the wind
how far would you search to rescue me

Whisper Ven Aqui

Took a picture while you slept
lying next to me
Havana
waves caressing time
dusk to dawn…kiss to kiss
as if I could forget the softness of you
at the break of dawn
lost emotions found

Whispering ven aqui
mi querida
I want you

Souvenirs of time side by side
a lifetime captured in just moments
Rio de Janeiro
moonlight touching sea
thunder to lightning…me touching you
as if I could forget hopscotch in the rain
ice cubes and honey
discovering true contentedness

Whispering ven aqui
mi querida
I need you

Felt your laughter surround all of me
feeling true and invincible love
Cape Town
sand held within the hourglass
heartbeat to heartbeat…you touching me
as if I could forget
showering within a waterfall
the magic of your magic kiss

Whispering ven aqui
mi querida…mi vida
I adore you

Double Dog Dare Ya

Gumboot heroes
splashing in the rain
two caped crusaders
bring the challenge on

wagon wheels in our pockets
a nickel buys the day
hide and seek
the adventure that we play

double dog dare ya
to be as brave
...as me

a budding buccaneer
swathed with yellow gumboots
a princess with a tiara demands purple
but then she is only four

stand by you forever
spit and hope to die
my word is my bond
what else do I have to give

double dog dare ya
to jump as high
...as me

no puddle ever too deep
no dream ever too far
a promise is a promise
don't ja know don't ja know

two untouched treasures
priceless trust and innocence
best friends forever
what else would best friends
...possibly be

Irish

Princesa

Com certeza
voce sabe agora
as palavras
forum ditos
com tanta facilidade
tambem meus segredos
transformaran nossa conversa
para saber de voce
foi para entender o amor
para tea mar-te
foi veradeiro meus cuidada

Eu sempre
vou me
preoculpar por ti
mis longe que entao
Princesa como sabia-te
tenho alguns segredos
no meio dia
quandos eu realizei
eu estava esperando
por te sozinho
eternamente pra sempre

Princess - Portugese

Princess

Of course
you know now
the words
were spoken
with such ease
my secret thoughts
became our conversation
that to know you
was to understand love
to love you
was to truly care

I will always
care for you
far more than I know
how not to
Princess do you know
I have been waiting
all of my life
for you alone
to love only you
it will always be
forever and a day

Flight

We pause
in flight
as if suspended clouds
arms outstretched
to the sky
as if imaginary
silver wings

Reaching far into
the unborn sunrises
of our lives
we are two
you and I
in total unison
side by side

The luxury
of trust
without fear
the splendour
of gentle love
our only wardrobe
the naked truth

Soaring in flight
parachutes not required
dreams shared as one
seatbelts discarded
for the safety
each others heartbeat
..up up and away

Shooting Stars

You had to know
our lives changed
forever at hello
you touched me
like a lightning bolt
I loved you completely
before the thunder rolled

My sweet sweet love
between the continents
and the seas
that separate us now
on my Irish soul
I miss you
with every breath

Please always always know
that every part
of you has touched
every part of me
I am but
the distance of
a wish from your side

Watch a shooting star
traverse the Southern Cross
and intimately know
we witness that journey as one
I claim that star in our name
my love if it takes forever
we will be together again

I believe that we are all poets at heart! I invite you to explore that part of your soul. If these poems engage you please feel free to write down your thoughts here. Nervous? Write those thoughts down as your secret and keep here within these pages...where they are forever safe! Or don't know how quite to get started? Why not take from this suggested sentence as a first line?;

"There was never a moment"

Write on my fellow scribe, write on! Please also feel free to contact me at my website: **www.thatcanadianpoet.com** and I would be happy to share thoughts on how to write what is in your heart!

Borderlines

Have you ever been at your borderline
met the right person…wrong place…wrong time
have you ever been taken to your knees
by a kiss so tender and forbidden
it took all that you were to simply let go

Have you ever loved someone so much
that you ignored the very essence of what you are
have you ever lied to someone you loved
and then felt them simply slip away
trust forsaken flees forever

Have you ever fallen in love with a stranger
have you ever loved someone who became a stranger
have you ever fallen into a self made chasm
past the point of turning back
having nothing and no one to hold onto

Have you ever sacrificed everything for love
to someone who then simply moved on
have you ever caught your own reflection
within your tear as it fell to the ground
looking at the face of a stranger

Have you ever been offered
everything that you ever wanted
at the price of everything you ever wanted
have you ever looked the other way
pretending no one else could see
… ….borderlines

Irish

Defaite

En un seul battement de coeur
avec votre doux sourire
vous avez croisé mon vide
écrasant
toute pensée de retraite

Ouvrant mon coeur
à votre intrusion sans effort
vous faisant confiance au-delà de toute raison
ayant besoin de vous
par-delà toute survie

Soudain ayant besoin seulement de vous
incontesté
audacieux
entièrement
et pour toujours vrai

Defeat - French

Defeat

In a single heartbeat
with your gentle smile
you crossed my void
smashing down
any thought of retreat

Opening my heart
to your effortless intrusion
trusting you past all reason
wanting you holding you
beyond all survival

Suddenly needing
this moment
with only you
unchallenged...daring
completely
and forever true

Loving You

There is a purpose in the truth of love
that lovers share between passion and twilight
the bond of love is sealed within a silken kiss
secrets are made to be kept…lies created only to be told

Life's journey is often bittersweet destiny the true hourglass
promises made in love are sworn at sunrise
remember …secrets rarely remain hidden
and lies can never be untold

Love is faith in the strength of the arms that hold you
time is the true gift of life and love is the test of truth shared
trust is believing in what we are and why we are one
to share and live out our dreams two as one

With my life I promise to protect you for all of my life
I will love you through all promises without condition
within you...beside you...for you...because of you…
my love my one true love come to me

Irish

City Souvenir

Departures, reservations and dreams
can all be changed
in a single wish, one heartbeat
we have shared so much
moments flowing within moments
souvenirs of that which
cannot be bought or sold

There is so much left
bridges to cross
our future to build
Sunday mornings busy
doing nothing at all
lovers within city limits
with no limit on love

Daybreak and dusk
free for the taking
ice chilled champagne
to warm the soul
the taste of summer rain
insatiable fragrance of true love
hot cappuccino sweet to the lips

You and I belong together
call this city home
take another plane
leave some other day
stay with me
I am yours to keep
a city souvenir

Un'eco Lontana

E' l'impossibile...sei forse tu
avevo avvertito la tua presenza solo qualche secondo prima
la dolcezza della tua voce
correva una volta ancora lungo il paesaggio della mia vita
raccogliendo tutta la passione
che ho solo conosciuto, assaporato e condiviso con te
così tanto tempo fa...una vita fa
la tua voce ... quella dolce voce piena di calore
che una volta dissolveva per me tutto il tempo di lei
una voce che con il solo suo soffice mormorio
strappava in un lampo qualunque resistenza
al desiderio...alla brama...di prendere e di dare
l'aroma della bramosia, della passione e di attimi fuori dal tempo
d'amore la perfetta trilogia...Amore a noi veniva sì spontaneo

Odoravo il tuo sentore profumato
come se la mia stessa vita ne dipendesse
ti stringevo fra le braccia la notte intera
come un uomo arenato stringe al petto la fiducia
il ricordo dei tuoi baci ancora mi perseguita
un bacio così esitante nella sua leggerezza che
già solo il ricordo mi scatena il pianto
ed ora, un'eco lontana di un passato proibito
ci salutammo per sempre in Italia tanto tempo fa
ma il tuo sapore è rimasto
sulle mie labbra come se mai il tuo tocco potesse finire
inimmaginabile...non si può mai davvero dire addio
a chi abbraccia i tuoi sogni
ti riduce in ginocchio...ancora e ancora

D'istinto mi volto per guardare quella falsa te
come osa imitare a perfezione
l'unica vera voce di passione nella mia vita
altre son passate da allora
non potrei mai mentirti
ma ho amato solo te amore mio ancora t'amo
E' l'impossibile...sei tu

Irish

A Distant Echo - Italian

A Distant Echo

It is the impossible…is it you
I had felt your presence seconds before
the softness of your voice
swept once again across my life's landscape
harvesting all of the passion that
I have only known, tasted and shared with you
so very long ago…a lifetime ago
your voice…that sweet warm voice
that once dissolved all of time herself for me
a voice whose soft murmur alone
could strip away any resistance in a heartbeat
to desire…to need…to take and to give
the scent of hunger, passion and timeless moments
love's perfect trilogy…amoré came so easily to us

I used to inhale your perfumed fragrance
as if my very life depended on it
I held you in my arms through the night
as a stranded man holds belief to his chest
thoughts of your kisses haunt me still
a kiss so staggeringly soft that
its memory alone brings tears to my eyes
and now, a distant echo from a forbidden past
we had said our goodbyes in Italy long ago
and yet the taste of you has lingered
on my lips as if your touch could never end
unimaginable…you can never truly say goodbye
to the one that enfolds your dreams
takes you to your knees…over and over

I turned instinctively to face the imposter
how dare she mimic to perfection
the one true voice of passion in my life
there have been others since
I could never lie to you
but l have loved only you and my love I do
it is the impossible…it is you

Irish

17

Dusk to Dusk

Summer

Reflections of the Spirit and Seasons of Love

Dockside Encounter

She took him in completely
that first day of July
walking across a dockside
capturing his soul
harnessing all of the gentle love
of an Irish man

In the second it takes
for a dream to come true
futures were decided
as easy as the rain
falls from the sky
two hearts became one

Once in a lifetime
a beautiful stranger beckons
and you answer
without challenge or fear
love arrives unannounced
and invites your soul to dance

On the side of a river
a day like so many others
except that everything you ever were
would be no more
a moment flows to you on a river
and carries your destiny beyond

Irish

Softer Moments

Where we run
I may not always be
and when we love
will not always be this free
day to day
night to morning star
give us the time
to take each day
seconds of softer moments
before rushing away

Looking back
knowing our moments
were only to hold
but never to stay
I loved you so
tender dreams
and gentle songs
tunes to which lovers
and their lovers
often play

Irish

Boston Pops

Early summer days in Boston
sunrise spent tracing Freedom Trail
the destiny of two begun
exploring the history of others
declarations of endless love

Crab cakes and tabasco
gentle laughter at daybreak
ice cold beer on tap… passion hot as flame
photographs taken
memories framed forever

Irish music and Boston cops
tall ships and walking the yard
begging for the shimmering heat to end
shared tables at Durgans Park
wanting your gentle kiss to never end…ever

Enchanted by the magic of Tanglewood
fireworks that dazzled at midnight
kisses that defied all resistance at dawn
Boston Pops…the Fourth of July…us
truly untouchable and delicious memories

Irish

Lifeguard

You alone knew
I was a long way
from my shore
a foot...a lifetime
reality is ruthlessly cold
there can be
desperately empty
times in your life

Deep water blues
nowhere to go

A sea of loneliness
simply unfathomable
to those who
pretend to believe
the abandoned heart
holds its rhythm
that lovers can always be
good friends for ever

Running on empty
no one to turn to

You alone knew
that waves of pain
have flowed through me
from dusk to dawn
I was drowning
no shoreline in sight
you reached for me
the lifeguard of my soul

Juegos de Verano

Que fue ayer
que me di cuenta de
que no volvían
me encontré el único espectador
el juego de los corazones
y el comodín se echó a reír con alegría en

Amor cancela en el recuento del dolor
el vencedor de nada en absoluto

Te pones tu sonrisa, así
como si fuera el uniforme de sus jugadores
lanzando promesas con luz de las velas
la captura de todas mis emociones suaves
por un breve momento
yo era tu jugador más valioso de

Juegas bien el juego
mejor de lo que podía

Summer Games – Spanish

Summer Games

It was only yesterday
that i realized
you were not coming back
I found myself the sole spectator
to the game of hearts
and the joker laughed on with glee

Love cancelled on the count of pain
the victor of nothing at all

You wear your smile well
as if it were your player's uniform
throwing out promises with candlelight
catching all of my gentle emotions
for one brief moment
I was your most valuable player

You play the game well
better than i ever could

Irish

Sandcastle Days

We tumble
with keys at the castle door
we tumble with each other
on the other side
love creates a glorious hunger

Idle afternoons spent
playing out a dream
that has come true
a princess soaring with superman
the ability to leap tall dreams

Savouring the sweet taste of love
warm gentle moments on the beach
building castles in the sand
looking beyond tomorrow
love with no boundaries

Intimately sensing
we are sharing love
as good as it gets
who knew that cornflakes
could taste this good

Irish

Heartbeats

Something happened
on the way to sunrise
you turned left
we turned wrong
now I am alone
wondering where
you are flying to tonight
did you know
so very little
of me

You ask questions
then refuse to hear the answers
there have been countless moments
when all we ever needed
we found in each other's eyes
do you not trust your heart beat
did you not trust mine
do you know
so very little
of yourself

Do you not recall
the echo of our heartbeats
each in total harmony to the other
is loving someone so
easy to do for you
and then so easy to undo
were we just imagination at play
did we know
so very little
of each other

No Way to Tell You

there is no way to tell you
how much you have changed my life
with just your smile
or in the quiet of the night
while your gentle breathing caresses
my body and soul

there is no way to thank you
for giving me back my life
how to explain your soft kiss
that I hunger for more
every sunrise lying
next to you

there is no way to replace
moments lost without you
time is too precious to throw away
and life and love is all about time
so please know my love
that I truly love you

there is no way to stop a clock
for if it were so
I would forever be allowed
one second frozen within eternity
as we sleep side by side
there is no way to tell you

Walking On Broken Glass

Thought that I knew all of the footsteps
that I would follow in the journey of my life
but the man in the moon smiled
and destiny asked my stars to dance
you turned my way… I felt my life change
the gentleness and honesty of our first kiss
feeling you reach into my inner-most soul
within seconds… needing you… wanting you forever

Pensei que conhecia todos os passos
que iria seguir em minha jornada
mas o homen na lua sorria
e o destino chamou nossas estrelas para dancar
voce mudou meu rumo… senti minha vida mudar
a suavidade e honestidade do nosso primerio beijo
que me fez sentir o seu toque no mais profundo de minha alma
precisando de voce querendo vocepara sempre e por um dia

Afternoons spent side by side
waves of emotion caught within shifting sand
passionate moments… tender dreams coming true
the hunger of a shared kiss… no one else can see
you stir my soul… you alone touch me like no one else
we have shared promises and confessions without words
you are the air that I breathe
I would walk on broken glass to be by your side

Irish

Second paragraph – Portugese

Passione

Il y a un but dans la vérité en amour
que partagent les amoureux entre la passion et le crépuscule
le lien de l'amour est scellé dans la douceur d'un baiser de papillon

Le temps est le vrai cadeau de la vie et l'amour
est l'épreuve de la vérité partagée
les promesses faites en amour ne sont pas écrites
elles sont jurées au lever du soleil
les secrets demeurent rarement cachés et les men-
songes ne peuvent jamais être retirés

L'amour est la foi dans la force des bras qui vous tiennent
la confiance c'est croire à ce que nous sommes et à pourquoi nous sommes un
pour partager vos rêves avec une âme sœur avec qui vous pouvez voler

Avec ma vie je promets de vous protéger toute ma vie durant
je vous aimerai au fil des promesses sans hésitation
en vous… près de vous… pour vous… en raison de vous

Irish

Passion - French

Passion

There is a purpose in the truth of love
that lovers share between passion and twilight
the bond of love is sealed within the gentleness of a butterfly kiss

Time is the true gift of life and love is the test of truth shared
promises made in love are not written they are sworn at sunrise
secrets rarely remain hidden and lies can never be untold

Love is faith in the strength of the arms that hold you
trust is believing in what we are and why we are one
to share your dreams with a soul-mate with whom you can fly

With my life I promise to protect you for all of my life
I will love you through all promises without hesitation
within you ... beside you...for you ... because of you

Irish

Michael B. Poyntz

Anam Cara

You are
my life
my bravery
my song
my joy

My sun
my dusk
my strength
my flower
my breath

My water
my star
my compassion
my calm
my fire

My air
my wind
my forgiveness
my warmth
my grace

My eternity
my sea
my gentleness
my laughter
my clay

My soul
my dawn
my fairness
my peace
my love

Irish

My Summer Mistress

I long for the soft easy moments of summer
resplendent with deliciously idle moments
but they have crept away
in the night
like a cat burglar
with all four paws
scratching at the skin
of an early fall
thoughts of favourite ice creams
overrun by leather bound diaries

Rich warm and luxurious sleep-ins
of a sultry August
overwhelmed by a distinctly cool change
between sunset and dawn
almost as if cellophane
has slipped within your skin
the intimate casualness of long walks
on Nantucket and 'the yard'
replaced by things to do
places to go

The promise of cool nights to come
protected by sentries of fire
old heavy sweaters
appear as if long lost friends
little consolation
to the empty hammock
one moment a dream machine
the next a piece of shipwrecked canvas
summer like a lusty mistress of the soul
moves on without a hint of regret

L'eco di Dentro

E' l'impossibile...sei tu
forse la crudele illusione di un'equa ricompensa
per aver fatto fesso il fesso che due anni fa ti ha sussurrato arrivederci
sono io ... l'estraneo che a Roma hai rapito col tuo sorriso
tu che ora sei solo a pochi centimetri da me e ancora sorridi
come ci riesci?...come ci si riesce, a farlo?
rubare un battito del cuore due volte in una vita
Italia terra di amore vino e risate
Dove gli amanti diventano artisti e l'amore è il loro capolavoro
creano paesaggi di passione tracciati sulla tela di un tramonto
baci dolci come sorbetti alla frutta, dal sapore irripetibile
dita colme di passione che esploravano la pelle come lava fusa
accendendo un fuoco annidato tanto nel profondo del tuo essere
che il calore dentro te sembra non avere fine

Da tramonto a tramonto sotto il dorato sole di Toscana
nude emozioni si facevano trasparenti come avvolte nel cellophane
dolcezza che lambiva l'ombelico della nostra stessa esistenza
innocenza e appetito...brama e tenerezza
condiviso amore che saluta la regina del desiderio
lei lussureggiante risponde come gocce di piog-
gia accarezzano mille foglie di loto
Venezia città galleggiante nascosta dietro un inganno mascherato
dove le sole vere verità che mai abbiamo conosciuto
le condividemmo con l'abbraccio in un'estate senza fine
il tempo ci volava accanto come la perpetua ombra del destino
era la frescura d'inizio autunno
che ci sussurrava dal bordo del fiume
giovani amanti è giunto il vostro momento di andar via
il vostro momento tornerà

Sai che ho offerto la mia anima?
la mia vita e tutto ciò che potrò mai essere
per sentire l'eco del tuo cuore che batte
stringimi l'anima un'ultima volta
affinché tu possa davvero sapere
che ho amata solo te e ancora t'amo
è l'impossibile...questo sono io

Irish

The Echo Within – Italian

The Echo Within

It is the impossible...it is you
perhaps the cruel illusion of a just reward
to fool the fool who whispered arrivederci to you years ago
it is me...the stranger in Rome you took with your smile
you who now stands barely inches away and smiles again
how do you do that...how does anyone do what you do
steal a heartbeat twice within a lifetime
Italy the land of amore wine and laughter
where lovers become artists and love is their masterpiece
creating landscapes of passion drawn on the canvas of a sunset
kisses as sweet as fruit sorbets whose flavours are unlike no other
fingertips so hot they explored skin like molten lava
creating a fire nestled deep in your core
that the heat within you seems to be endless

Dusk to dusk spent under a golden Tuscan sun
raw emotions became transparent as if wrapped in cellophane
tenderness that licked the nexus of our very existence
innocence and hunger...need and gentleness
shared love that beckons to the mistress of lust
whose lush reply is like raindrops caressing a thousand lotus leaves
Venice a city afloat hiding behind masked deception
where the only truths we have ever known
we shared in each other's arms through an endless summer
time slipped by as if the perpetual shadow of destiny
it was the coolness of the early fall
that whispered to us by the river's edge
young lovers your time to go has arrived
your time will come again

Do you know that I have offered my soul
my very life and all that I would ever be
to feel the echo of your heartbeat
hold my soul one last time
that you might truly know
I have loved only you and I do
it is the impossible...this is me

Irish

35

Dusk to Dusk

Fall

Reflections of the Spirit and Seasons of Love

Inside Out

Some words need to be shared…and passion taken
to where there are no words
there are feelings that turn you inside out
there is nothing left to say
deep inside where
no one ever seems to touch the real you
your soul-mate need only to beckon
come be with me…forever

and you do
you always will

There are kisses offered unto eternity
forever and a day
a sense of satisfaction beyond description
you simply hunger for one more
deep inside where no one ever seems to know the real you
your soul-mate simply whispers
stand with me…forever

you always will
and you do

Irish

Bend Down and Touch Me

Called you up this morning
from halfway around the world
needed to feel your voice
hold my heart one more time
unwrapped you from your silken dream
and took you deep inside of mine

Heard your easy smile
when I asked you
to fly down to the coast
I need to be with you again
a week-end lost finding each other
somewhere…somehow

Forgive the time and distance
I have placed between us
searching for what I already held
wrapped in your arms
a fool's search…led by a fool

I love you more
than words or promises
could ever say
somehow I will find you
bend down and touch
me with your smile
I need to be with you again

Chocolate

There is a purpose in the truth
lovers share between passion and twilight
the bond of love is sealed with the belief in forever
with my life I promise to protect you with all of my life

Love takes you as you are…
                        …to where you have never been

Secrets in life are made only to be kept…lies only to be told
love can let you touch the sun…love can take you to your knees
promises made in love are promises of truth and promises of time
secrets rarely remain hidden and lies can never be untold

Love has the power of forgiveness…
                        …the sweetness of chocolate

Love is faith in the strength of the arms that you run to
trust is believing in what we are uniquely etched within the other
sharing the dreams of butterfly kisses…touching you
within you…beside you…for you…because of you

        now and forever   dusk to dusk

Irish

Melissa

I looked
for you today
far across
our empty crowded room
wanting…needing
to tell you
that I was truly sorry

For Melissa
for even lover's dreams
fall prey
to the morning sun

All we wanted
was each other
and time
first true love
discovered and lost
I miss you

Tirar Uma Foto

Enquanto você dormia
dentro da sua docura
do sol de manhã
como eu nunca vou esquecer
a pureza extasiado
de està perdido dentro de voce

Tendecia de capturar
dentro do raio do sol
o beijo taõ doce
vai ser pra sempre
hesitar sobre meus láabios
pra sempre um dia

Tira uma foto
enquanto você dormia
tente me capturar
um perfeito momento
dois coracaŏ batendo num só
como eu naŏ poderia nunca esquecer
o arrepio do sabor
do amor com voce alvorecer

Took A Picture – Portugese

Took A Picture

Took a picture
while you slept
trying to capture the magic
of you your soft breathing
to hold it forever
a second etched within eternity

Savoring the total rapture
of moments spent
lying by your side

Tenderness captured
like a cascading waterfall
amazingly gentle passion
teasing my every sensation like twilight
touching every corner of my universe

The sheer lustrous hunger
of tasting your love
dusk to dawn

Took a picture
while you slept
held within the morning light
as if I could ever
forget this moment
my everlasting love for you

Irish

Michael B. Poyntz

Original Hand Written Poem

1

Promise

take me back
across the Bay
to Sausalito
and other times
when we could
get lost
within a gallery
and I
lost within
them am you
Sometimes when
I long
for those moments
with you.
once again
            Michael

2

I will pass
this way again
surrendering the logic
and reason
to an afternoon
spent
in Frisco
learning,
that you too.
wake-up
alone.
and wonder why.
            Michael

Multiple choice poem solution.

44

Friends Lover and Strangers

Crayons and movies
strawberry shortcake for two
these are things
that belong to me and you
whispers and seaside
a time by the bay

Days to hours
things that come what may

Airports, highways … reasons
something always between us
our closest companion…distance
as our common bond
memories and moments of you
lay deep within my soul

Hours to minutes
things that come what may

Friends lovers and strangers
we became three as one
forgiving and needing
the softness of you and the sun
more for us was not to be
never truly knowing why

Minutes to seconds
things that come what may

Sunset to dusk
and all the moments
in between…we were free
and now that the years
have swept time away
like a tide beckoned by the sea

Seconds to heartbeats
I live for you every day

The Wizard of Dreams

Is that truly you
knocking on my door
arriving one stroke past midnight
one dreamer seeking another
chasing the clouds in a cloudless sky
riding a flying carpet
with no horizon in sight

Is that truly me
playing out the game
of lover's chance
waiting for the curtain call
my audience has arrived
the wizard of dreams
in the seat of wishful thinking

Is that truly us
are we just strangers
standing at destiny's edge
witnessing two lives come and go
each and all simply waiting
for the crystal ball of chance
to arrive unbroken

Is this all there is
were we both expecting
there would be more
the swan and the song perhaps
to fulfill all expectations
challenging the dreamer in our souls
to a dual of lover's risk
.....truly

Irish

Don't Count on Sunshine

The face in the moon
looked over her shoulder
and whispered to you
you ask for too much
for that which may never be
why don't you smell the clover
ride the red rocket
race to touch the sky
truly celebrate this day
you never know if sunshine
will come your way again

Truly seize this day
run as fast and as far as you can
love as if you were thirsty water
pretend that you are the wind
hold the hands of the ones
who love you closely to your heart
what will be will be
play hopscotch ..eat ice cream
covet and celebrate this hour
you never know if sunshine
will come your way again

You look to the stars
to fulfil dreams of more
don't you know you have so much
love is everything and you have it
you are the master of
your very dreams
savour the gift called happiness
value good health as if it were gold
truly celebrate this minute
you never know if sunshine
will come your way again

Your family and friends
live to see your smile
tell them they are everything to you
you who is never happy
even with your own reflection
destiny has given you much and yet
you dream simply to have more
remember even rainbows can fade away
truly celebrate this heartbeat
you never know if sunshine
will come your way again

Michael B. Poyntz

Promesses

Je ne cours plus
apres les promesses
mais cela n'a rien
de surprenant
je ne croirai
jamais plus aux promesses

Une fois il n'y pas si longtemps
quelqu'un a promis
de partager une centaine
de jours et une centaine de reves
mais aujourd'hui les jours
et les reves s'en sont alles

A mes propres mots
je n'y crois plus
pourquoi ces promesses
inachevees
sont-elles les plus
marquees dans nos memoires

Irish

Promises – French

Promises

I don't look
for promises anymore
but that is not
really surprising
I don't keep
promises anymore either

Not so long ago
someone promised
to share a thousand days
and a thousand dreams
but now those days
and dreams have all gone

Can someone tell me
do the words I do
really mean I won't
why is it that promises
never last as long
as the memories

Irish

Hear All About It

If we were tomorrow's headline
would we be missing lovers
reported as lost without a trace
or simply declared guilty
by the court of hearts and souls
traitors to the quest of love

Have our stories to each other
simply become yesterday's news
like day old doughnuts
cheaper by the dozen

There was a time my love
when we planned our very lives
on paper napkins
dreams were all that we could afford
the promise of fame and fortune mere gossip
every sunrise a fresh new edition

My Closet Door

what answers do you need to quell your curiosity
do you so doubt the truth of our first kiss
have you watched so long that you no longer see me
what secrets did you think i would hide from you
for you alone have undressed me to bare flesh

is it my collection of unpolished shoes
the legacy of footsteps taken to life's other doorways
that troubles you so
do you think i would not stand by you now
when every second of my being is all about our future

what puzzles to life's mysteries
will be answered by the echo of silent voices
held within pages of dusty photograph albums
aged moments haunt you as if they were immortal
mirror snapshots of strangers smiling for strangers

images created in a world requiring its own reflection
is it my hat boxes with no labels holding silent accords
that you so desperately need to renounce out loud
i recall moments when your gentle movement inside of me
was the only sound needed to tell the world we were one

were you looking for a suitcase packed with excuses
a ticketless boarding pass for a blameless departure
do you fear sunrise without my dreams to protect you
sunset with no one to believe in no one to hold you
we have crossed the world's longitudes and latitudes

Rio to Monterrey…Brisbane to Berlin
we have known love dusk to dawn….again and again
what i have shared with you
i have shared with no one else…no one
listen to me ..hear me…this is the voice of your destiny

Irish

L'eco Dell' Oltre

Era l'impossibile ... dirsi addio
la vita mi chiedeva troppo
a Roma le nostre esistenza cambiarono per sempre
il tuo sorriso mi toccava
con l'elettricità di un fulmine
ti ho amata completamente in quel primo istante
ti amo adesso
nulla è mai più stato
lo stesso per me senza te
non senti il mio cuore battere
dentro ad ogni alba e ogni crepuscolo
da tramonto a tramonto?

Fra un'eco lontana
e l'eco di dentro delle nostre vite
avevo trovato e poi ho perduto
il mio solo grande amore
non potrei mai lasciarti andare ancora
amore mio ti chiedo adesso
di stare per sempre al mio fianco

Amore mio tu sei la mia stessa anima
ogni parte del tuo cuore
vive in ogni battito del mio
con l'ineluttabilità di ogni onda dell'oceano
che non può lambire che una sola sponda
noi siamo l'uno dell'altra
quello che sembrava impossibile
deve ora piegarsi e cedere
alla promessa del destino di tanto tempo fa
i nostri giorni nel sole
ci vengono offerti di nuovo
questo è il possibile
siamo tu ed io

The Echo Beyond – Italian

The Echo Beyond

It was the impossible...to bid farewell
life asked too much of me
our lives changed forever in Rome
you touched me with your smile
like a lightning bolt
I loved you completely at that first moment
I love you now
nothing has ever been
the same for me without you
have you not felt my heartbeat
within each sunrise and sunset
dusk to dusk

Between a distant echo
and the echo within our lives
I had found and then lost
my one true love
I could never let you go again
mi amoré I ask now to you
to stay by my side forever

My love you are my very soul
every part of your heart
lives within every heartbeat of mine
as surely as each wave in the ocean
is destined to touch but one shore
we belong together
that which seemed impossible
must now bow down and yield
to destiny's promise of long ago
our days in the sun
are granted once more
this is the possible
it is you and me

Dusk to Dusk

Winter

Reflections of the Spirit and Seasons of Love

My Hero's Song

In my eyes
you have always been
my true hero
always there for me
no matter where or why
without question
not seeking an answer
you are the loyalty instinctive to me

In my life
you have always challenged me
as the mentor of my truths
teaching me to stand tall
against the wind... at times alone
to believe in myself
and to never surrender...ever
you are the strength within me

In my world
your gentleness touches me
protecting me from all of harm's way
with unwavering and eternal courage
teaching me to implicitly know
true love is unconditional
asking only belief in return
you are the truth about me

In my soul
you are the gift of a thousand rainbows
my best friend unto infinity
the one who truly watches over me
please know...that I forever know
I am the true reflection of you
in this we will always be
two as one...one as two

I am truly the very best of you

Irish

I Need To Hear It

How long have you shared
your secret lover with the world
the one you kept from my ears
did you decide to move on
last night while we made love
or was it this morning
when I still had reason
to believe in you

Perhaps it was Sunday
as I cleaned the rooms
while you walked the dog

How long have I been
your excuse to leave early

Where in the world
did you promise to travel to
as I made your favorite bread

I need to hear it from you
how a life time spent by my side
has lost its meaning to you
what covenants were made
as you broke
all of your covenants made to me
you will never know
the safety of my kiss again

Poem to Magee

There was
a moment
an incredible second
when I dared to cross
the invisible line
built with such great care
between us
to protect
our gentle
silent secrets

How could i know
there would only be
one of you

And yet
in a single heartbeat
devoid of reason
or restraint
I crossed into your world
discovering you
my first true love
within my grasp
and within
my life

How would I know
there could only be
one of you

Irish

I Will Always Be Here

when you look for me
my love
look to the direction
of the wind
i will surround you
with the scent of trust

when you hunger for me
my love
reach out for the rising sun
i will fill your heart
with the warmth of love

when you need to be held
my love
turn to the tide
that comes to the shore
i will be there
with all that I am

when you think of me
my love
turn to the light
of the moon
i will be beside you
as close as a whisper

Cada Vez Mas

Hace mucho tiempo
en un lugar llamado
mi memoria
que llegó a
hasta el momento en mí
como si solo
siempre ha sostenido
la contraseña secreta
a mi alma más interna

Me encantó, a continuación,

Toda una vida
en un castillo llamado
mi corazón
me entregué a ser
siempre a tu lado
tu alma
las minas para proteger a
para que usted se había desbloqueado
misterios de la vida para mí

Te amo ahora

Un latido del corazón hace
en un lugar llamado
nuestro hogar
te vi dormir
y dio
gracias silencio
para cada sueño
que sólo usted
han hecho realidad

Te amaré
... ... cada vez más

Irish

Evermore - Spanish

Evermore

A long time ago
in a place called
my memory
you reached
so far into me
as if you alone
had always held
the secret password
to my innermost soul

I loved you then

A lifetime ago
in a castle called
my heart
I surrendered to be
forever by your side
your very soul
mine to protect
for you had unlocked
life's mysteries for me

I love you now

A heartbeat ago
in a place called
our home
I watched you sleep
and gave
silent thanks
for every dream
that you alone
have made come true

I will love you
… …evermore

Irish

The Truth of Consequences

Have you ever
caught someone you love
in a lie that they whispered
suddenly
a lifetime of conversations
past and present
is no longer
and can no longer be
the same again
.....ever

So much history
cast to the wind
for so little
a promise once forgotten
become's unforgettable
the difference between
 a lie that you hear
and the truth

Is every thing
you ever were
.....forever

Have you ever
been caught by someone you love
in a lie that you whispered
suddenly
a lifetime of dreams
present and future
will never be
and can never be
 the same again
.....ever

So much future
lost to the wind
for so little
a covenant once vanquished
becomes unforgiveable
the difference between
a lie that you tell
and the truth

Is everything
you will never be
.....forever

The Sound of Silence

There was nothing
left to say
perhaps the silence
is all we need to hear
each word … every word
one word too many

Attempts to justify
half truths
and full lies
in a world full of noise
the sound of silence
is a welcome reprieve

You ask for the truth
to be declared out loud
my love I have spoken
with each and every kiss
countless whispers
of my trust in you

Winter.....the time of reflection! Nights are longer and colder! At this point I urge you to reach inside your heart, your memories your true feelings and etch those words on this page! Write them as they come to you! If you have ever wanted to capture the words in your heart and pass them on to someone you care for...then do it here, do it today!

Then sign that poem and give this book with your signed poem on the inside.

How to start such a poem?....try this:

"I love you..I always have
you are everything to me
my sunrise and sunset
every single day"

Write on my fellow scribe, write on! Please feel free to contact me at my website: **thatcanadianpoet.com** and I would be happy to share ideas and thoughts on how to write what is in your heart! When done....you sign it and give 'Dusk to Dusk' to that person who truly touches your life!

I Never Knew

I never knew
love could hurt you
through and through
ransacking your very core
shattering the truth of trust
the weight of a single teardrop
can take the strongest to their knees

I never knew
passion can be a two-edged sword
one side shining so brightly
it blinds all rhyme and reason
the other merciless in its swath
your body and soul cut to pieces
no longer recognizable

I never knew
that being left behind
devastates everything
all that you hold dear in life
vanishes like winter snow
the pain of loneliness
has no equal

I never knew
the lover in your arms
once beckoned by the call of destiny
will leave as surely as the morning tide
must flow from the bay
that which is not to be
can never ever be

but now I know

Au Revoir Mon Amor

Je vous ai senti vous éloigner
et j'ai su que les mots
vous appelant à revenir
n'étaient plus les miens à crier

moments et mémoires
visions brouillées d'hier

cela que j'ai gardé comme notre toujours
ne fait plus partie de mon lendemain

je vous ai observé vous en aller doucement
sachant intimement
que je devais prendre
un chemin séparé

Irish

Good Bye My Love - French

Good Bye My love

I felt you pull away
and knew that the words
calling you back
were no longer mine to cry out

Moments and memories
blurred visions of yesterday

That which I held as our forever
no longer part of my tomorrow

I watched you drift away
intimately knowing
that I was to take
a separate path

I will always miss you

Irish

Just Move On - Lyrics

Do what you are going to do
say what you are going to say, baby
then move on out of my life
take what ever you want , baby
we both know I mean nothing to you
your are not the one I trust anymore
but you used to be

Move to the far edge of town
run to the other side of goodbye
just move on ...out of my life
call whoever you want, baby
call who ever you need
we both know I mean nothing to you
your not the one I want anymore
but you used to be

I only wanted you to be true
sharing two lives living under one roof
baby baby that is something
you just won't do
it breaks my heart
for what I have to say
one of us is leaving here today
baby baby
just move on
without me

Just Move On - Lyrics

Do what you want to do
play the games you always play
then move on out of my life
lie to the man in the moon, baby
lie to the face in your mirror
but you wil never lie to me again
your promises are not what I need anymore
but they used to be

Pack my suitcase full of your lies
take your shirts and your alibis
just move on out of my life
take a cab or climb on a jet plane
sit on the corner or stand in the rain
you are not the one I run to anymore
but you used to be

I only wanted you to be true
sharing two lives living under one roof
baby baby that is something
you just won't do
it breaks my heart
for what i have to say
one of us is leaving here today
baby baby
just move on
without me

Irish

All Rights Reserved

Polvere in Frantumi

Ho chiuso con te
per tutto quanto importa
questo è certo
ho chiuso con te
anche per tutto quanto importa di meno
se non contiamo il fatto che
mi ritrovo in ginocchio
ogni volta
...che respiro

Tutto me stesso
la mia vita voltata
e rivoltata
da te
e le tue bugie
come è stato possibile
che così tanto di me
volesse dire così poco
...per te

Non è abbastanza
le scuse che implorano perdono
per l'imperdonabile
ciò che ho sempre
creduto vero
ha tradito la mia anima
la mia fiducia in me
l'ha frantumata sino a farne polvere
...credere in chi ora

Irish

Shattered Dust - Italian

Shattered Dust

I am over you
in all the big ways
that is for sure
I am over you
in all the small ways too
if you don't count
going to my knees
with each moment
...that I breathe

All of me
my life turned around
over and over
by you
and your lies
how could
so much of me
mean so little
...to you

It is not enough
excuses seeking forgiveness
for the unforgiveable
what I have always
held to be true
betrayed my very soul
my trust in me
shattered to dust
...trust who now

Irish

Dawn to Dawn

Excerpts of selected poems from this
collection to be released fall 2010

Michael B. Poyntz

Dedicated to the Inauguration of President Barak Obama

I Want

Mankind to be kinder to man
the world to echo the belief "yes we can"
for children to live without fear
to know literacy and opportunity
equality to be truly equal
life to be valued higher than gold

The tally of ones true legacy
to be measured by their mercy
law to always speak the truth
a right to offer prayer to be absolute
the plague of racism to be vanquished
earth's bounty to feed the hungry

The games we play called war
to be declared forever over
the blindness of all hate
to be granted sight and tolerance
the cries of the weak and abused
to be answered by the strong

Our rain forests to be cherished
whales to roam free within pristine seas
the words spoken ''never again''
to never again be needed to be said
every man to be a brother of mine
each child to be my child

Within my lifetime

Irish

Gifts Within Your Lifetime

I offer you a vase
to hold the memories of your dusk to dawn
to fill with coins
for the days that you share with those who have none
to fill with flowers
for the days to remind you of natures beauty
to fill with strength
for the days that you will need to be strong
to fill with the generosity of the heart
for the days that you are called to forgive
to fill with the smell of the sea
for the days that you stand on the desert
to fill with dreams
for the days that your hopes are shattered
to fill with the richness of eternal friendship
for the days that you will be called to stand alone
to fill with magic
for the days you need to fly and touch the sun
to fill with sweet memories
for the days that are painful to forget
to fill with your truths
for the days that others lie to you
to fill with the closeness of my heartbeat
for the days you need to be held

Irish

古漢語熟語

我們不能保證在生活中
救人一..., 沒有我們
當然不是我, 可能不是你
沒有人能夠逃脫呼籲自己的命運
從一個說法
只有通過建立律師

不要依賴於幸運餅乾
為理由, 辭掉工作

吃辛辣食物中
一個紙箱內用筷子... ...更頻繁
坐在公園的長椅和交談的孤獨陌生人
說這些話的日常
感謝你... ... ..請...。, 我愛你
因為如果他們真的在乎的你

請你自己仔細線在沙
然後捍衛他們的所有, 您的

喝熱咖啡的碗
守住一個你愛的雙手
無論你在生活中做了強烈的熱情
永遠做你的敵人
希望你永遠做...
生活得更好的愛 ...

當你覺得你在最危險
真正知道的是, 第二危險的臨近給你
跳舞, 唱你的心做好每一天
活...。只是生活一樣大, 你可以
記住阿拉莫
愛爾蘭文

寫在範她嗯咖啡廳 - 2010年2月
維多利亞的最佳中餐

Irish
Old Chinese Sayings - Cantonese

Old Chinese Sayings

There are no guarantees in life
save one…and none of us
certainly not me and possibly not you
no one can outrun the call of their own destiny
once upon a time is a saying
created only by the lawyers

Don't rely on fortune cookies
as the reason to quit your job

Eat spicy Chinese food
out of a carton …with chopsticks…more often
sit on a park bench and talk with a lonely stranger
say these words daily
thank you… …..please….and I love you
as if they actually mattered to you

Draw your own lines carefully in the sand
then defend them with all that you are

Drink hot coffee from a bowl
hold onto the one you love with both hands
whatever you do in life do it with intense passion
never do what your enemy
expects you to do…ever
live well …love better

When you feel you are in the least danger
be truly aware for it is at that second danger draws near to you
dance and sing your heart out every single day
live….just live as large as you can
remember the Alamo

Irish

Written at the Fan Tan Cafe – February 2010

Victoria's Best Chinese food

Michael B. Poyntz

On the Rocks

Scotch and love on the rocks
both hard to swallow

One can bring tears to the eyes
the other tears from the heart

One easy to walk away from
the other impossible to outdistance

One mellows with time
the other will always feel like just a moment ago

One takes you gently
the other can take you to your knees

One easy to look forward to
the other can take you completely by surprise

One allows you to toast your fortune
the other a treasure lost

One may take a day to get over
the other you may never get over

One can be done alone or with strangers
the other takes just two

One can be stirred
the other can shake your very soul

One is measured by age alone
the other can happen regardless of age

One is referred to with words of respect
the other of words you wish you had never said

You get to choose the one
from the other

Irish

Let the Mercy Begin

There is pain in the city today Lord
tears came with the morning wind
I'm down on my knees
searching for my brothers and my sisters
promises of forever changed forever in a moment
let the mercy begin

Dreams of tomorrow are now yesterday's memories
families lost with strangers...life lost with innocence
kiss them softly for they have suffered
protect them all from harm's way
let them be forever warm
let the mercy begin

Planes flew through the sky right to heavens gate
a nations strength now resolved from the dust of towers
the price of freedom paid for in full on a country field
fortress warriors taken without quarter
lay each one of them so softly and gently down
let the mercy begin

A choir of heroes each one a protector of life
men and women who answered every plea for help
brave comrades falling in the flames as many to save the few
let their heartbeats become heaven's eternal sweet symphony
allow our lives to be a reflection of their true courage and spirit
let the mercy begin

Our distance apart is now but a breath of time
to find one another...simply reach to the sun
in the sound of a child's laughter
and when I yearn for the gentleness of their touch
I will need only to hold a butterfly in my hands
let the mercy begin

Irish

*Written and Dedicated to the New York City Fire
Departments September 15th , 2001*

Thirsty Water

I should have gone to work today but
your tongue convinced me to come
inside and play with you...to ride our
red rocket ship to the distant planet of
lust where sensual sins are instantly
forgiven and forgotten amidst the mute
pleas for gentle mercy so rightly ignored
as a gesture to rationality and begging for more
is of course granted by the Court of No Regret

You alone have always held the secret
key that released the chastised prisoner of
passion locked so deep inside of me...your taste
buds have caressed every morsel of my
body as if I were an ice cube wrapped
in honey much like the oyster swallowed
whole to tease our ravaged pendulums whose
demand for thirsty water shall be quenched at the
moment our tongues mysteriously turn ice cold

Irish

Thirsty Sea

the indelible scent of ecstasy filled their auras with the
fragrance of lovemaking spent and aroused passion anxious to
be tasted then devoured...skin forged on skin...a magical
collaboration of need satisfying need...moments when love
takes you far beyond reality...no limits... no borders...nothing refused...
your physical surrender a mere formality as flesh seeks flesh...
frolicking taste-buds unlocking rivers of dreams whose surge simply wash
away the pain of loveless droughts...in a heartbeat forever forgotten
all resistance simply ripped away as flame licks ice as if it were
candy... mouths drawn to loins scented by eucalyptus that
once inhaled becomes unforgettable and forevermore addic-
tive as the taste of warm summer honey cloaks the soul
the strength of passion is found in it's gentleness the luxury of being touched
so deeply...so intimately your soul is turned inside out...eager to respond
the relentless tongue victoriously plays hide and seek as a master...once
found you beg for the mercy of more you are never the same again...ever...
as if a thirsty sea lay within your soul and it's tide is forever restless paradise
found ...over and over...emptiness abandoned as if a decree by the gods
of love...two scent's becoming one..the air you breathe forever shared...
the promise of forever scratched on your skin as if you were a trophy

Irish St Paddy's Day 2010

Michael B. Poyntz

Steinbeck's California Town

Part of me my love
will always miss
that part of you
surrendered to my heart
the first time
we made love
beside Monterey Bay
the morning sun was on the rise
as all of the walls of our defenses
came down..brick by brick
kiss by kiss

I fell in love with you
more than I knew possible
in Steinbeck's California town

Three days by a bay
long hot showers for two
a room we might forget one day
passion so deep... so intense
we could never forget...ever
lost soul mates discovered
side by side. heartbeat within heartbeat
walking beside an ice cold sea
shared kisses hot as flame
we owned... those days
priceless moments and memories

I love you more now
than I ever thought possible
in Steinbeck's California town

Irish

ABOUT THE AUTHOR

Canadian born writer, poet and lyricist Michael B. Poyntz has written poetry for all of his adult life. Signing under his nomme de plume 'Irish' became part of his writing identity and style in the early 70's while studying in Toronto. Michael's public readings have been warmly received across North America including memorable appearances at the acclaimed 'Busboy and Poets', Washington, DC! When not traveling to present his poems in front of audiences he resides in an oceanside cottage on the stunningly beautiful Vancouver Island, Canada. He continues to write and create as part of his daily journey.

To find out more about 'That Canadian Poet' publications; posters; unique gifts; public performance dates and locations go to **www.thatcanadianpoet.com** or contact direct at **thatcanadianpoet@shaw.ca.**